Introducing the SAS® System

Version 6
First Edition

SAS Institute Inc.
SAS Campus Drive
Cary, NC 27513

The correct bibliographic citation for this manual is as follows: SAS Institute Inc., *Introducing the SAS® System, Version 6, First Edition*, Cary, NC: SAS Institute Inc., 1991. 83 pp.

Introducing the SAS® System, Version 6, First Edition

The SAS® System is an integrated system of software providing complete control over data access, management, analysis, and presentation. Base SAS software is the foundation of the SAS System. Products within the SAS System include SAS/ACCESS®, SAS/AF®, SAS/ASSIST®, SAS/CPE®, SAS/DMI®, SAS/ETS®, SAS/FSP®, SAS/GRAPH®, SAS/IML®, SAS/IMS-DL/I®, SAS/OR®, SAS/QC®, SAS/REPLAY-CICS®, SAS/SHARE®, SAS/STAT®, SAS/CONNECT™, SAS/DB2™, SAS/INSIGHT™, SAS/SQL-DS™, and SAS/TOOLKIT™ software. Other SAS Institute products are SYSTEM 2000® Data Management Software, with basic SYSTEM 2000, CREATE™, Multi-User™, QueX™, Screen Writer™, and CICS interface software; NeoVisuals® software; JMP®, JMP IN®, and JMP Serve™ software; SAS/RTERM® software; and the SAS/C® Compiler. MultiVendor Architecture™ and MVA™ are trademarks of SAS Institute Inc. *SAS Communications®, SAS Training®, SAS Views®,* and the SASware Ballot® are published by SAS Institute Inc. All trademarks above are registered trademarks or trademarks, as indicated by their mark, of SAS Institute Inc.

A footnote must accompany the first use of each Institute registered trademark or trademark and must state that the referenced trademark is used to identify products or services of SAS Institute Inc.

The Institute is a private company devoted to the support and further development of its software and related services.

DEC™, Rdb/VMS™, and VMS™ are trademarks of Digital Equipment Corporation. IBM® and OS/2® are registered trademarks and DB2™ is a trademark of International Business Machines Corporation. ORACLE® is a registered trademark of Oracle Corporation. UNIX® is a registered trademark of AT&T.

Doc S8, Ver111.0N, 041591

Contents

Credits

Documentation

Composition	Eloise M. Currie, Candy R. Farrell, Blanche W. Phillips, Denise L. Truelove
Graphic Design	Creative Services Department
Proofreading	Patsy P. Blessis, Carey H. Cox, Paramita Ghosh, Toni P. Sherrill, John M. West, Susan E. Willard
Technical Review	Miguel Bamberger, Claudia Cavedon, Art Cooke, Betsy Corning, Anne Corrigan, Ottis R. Cowper, Steve Darbyshire, Michelle Fruchtenicht, Shirley N. Garrett, B. Claire McCullough, Jens Dahl Mikkelsen, Duane E. Ressler, Cindy Swamp, Mogens Weinreich
Writing and Editing	Caroline Brickley, Christina N. Harvey, Jeffrey Lopes, Gary R. Meek

CHAPTER 1

Introducing the SAS® System

The power, flexibility, breadth, and ease-of-use of the SAS System are designed to help your organization gain complete control of your most strategic asset—your data. The SAS System can take data, in any form and from any source or location, and enable users in your organization to manipulate those data according to their needs and level of computing expertise to produce information that is both accurate and meaningful.

This chapter describes the features that make the SAS System an integrated applications system. These features include

☐ total control of your data

☐ flexible user interfaces

☐ integration of computing environments

☐ ability to package complete applications.

Why Do You Need the SAS System?

Understanding your data is crucial to understanding your business.

As an information manager, you face a number of challenges:

- ☐ Your data are often distributed throughout your organization, creating disconnected islands of information.

- ☐ Your staff have different levels of computer experience, from new users to experienced programmers.

- ☐ Your organization develops applications for every phase of its business, from research to manufacturing to personnel.

- ☐ Your diverse hardware systems make integration of your computing environment difficult.

The SAS System gives you the tools for managing your most important resources: people and data.

To make your organization most productive, the SAS System

- ☐ gives you control over data access, management, analysis, and presentation in one integrated software system

- ☐ accommodates the skill levels of its users, reducing the learning curve for new users and providing power and flexibility for more experienced users

- ☐ satisfies a wide range of applications needs, from finance and sales to decision support to research and testing

- ☐ provides a full inventory of applications development tools

- ☐ facilitates applications that run in more than one computing environment, preserving your investment in existing hardware and software and giving you the freedom to add new technologies.

The SAS System offers a strategic solution.

The SAS System is strategic for your information delivery and applications development needs because it integrates all of these elements into one powerful, flexible, and easy-to-use software system.

How Can You Gain Total Control of Your Data?

The SAS System provides control of the four basic data-centered tasks:

With any body of data, you must perform four basic tasks to make it useful and meaningful information. Your data are at the center of four basic tasks: access, management, analysis, and presentation. These four data-driven tasks are common to every application you develop for your business.

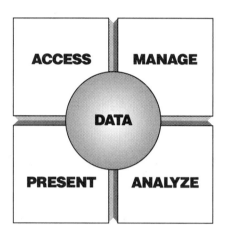

☐ **access**

You need to get to your data quickly and efficiently. The SAS System enables you to access data for use in your applications, no matter how or where they are stored or in what format the data exist.

☐ **management**

Data are rarely in the form you need them. Once you access data through the SAS System, you can use its data management features to update, rearrange, combine, edit, or subset the data before analyzing them.

☐ **analysis**

Data analysis lets you discover what all the facts mean, helping you make decisions necessary to keep your business moving forward. The tools for analysis range from simple descriptive statistics to more advanced or specialized analyses.

☐ **presentation**

Having the facts is only part of the answer. You must communicate what you have learned from them. Data presentation capabilities range from simple lists and tables to multidimensional plots to elaborate full-color graphics on many types of media.

What Interfaces Are Available for New Users?

The SAS System provides flexible user interfaces.

A user interface is a way to create and run SAS applications. By providing a variety of interfaces, the SAS System enables both the novice user and the most experienced SAS programmer to control all four data-centered tasks.

SAS/ASSIST software is a menu-driven, task-oriented interface.

SAS/ASSIST menus enable you to select keywords to perform tasks such as managing data, printing a report, or creating graphics. New SAS users can use the SAS/ASSIST interface to develop applications without learning the syntax of the SAS language because SAS/ASSIST software actually builds and stores SAS programs as menu selections are made. More experienced users can use SAS/ASSIST programs as a base for customized applications that run independently or within the SAS/ASSIST environment.

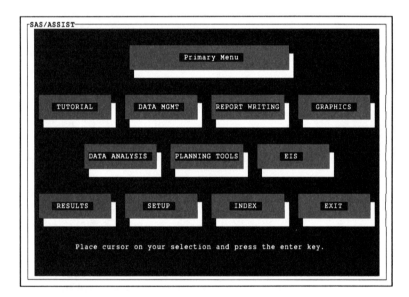

Two books provide more information on using the SAS System through the SAS/ASSIST menus:

☐ *SAS/ASSIST Software: Your Interface to the SAS System, Version 6, First Edition*

☐ *Getting Started with the SAS System Using SAS/ASSIST Software, Version 6, First Edition.*

What Interfaces Are Available for Experienced Users?

The SAS Display Manager System is a convenient programming environment.

You can also develop SAS applications by writing SAS programs. The SAS Display Manager System is an interactive windowing system that enables you to write and modify your programs, run them, and monitor the output and messages. Its convenient pull-down menus simplify routine file management tasks.

The display manager interface can be customized.

You can use menus or type commands on a command line to display windows, alter their size, shape and placement on the display, edit text, and search for words and phrases. The display below shows the flexibility you have in customizing display manager windows.

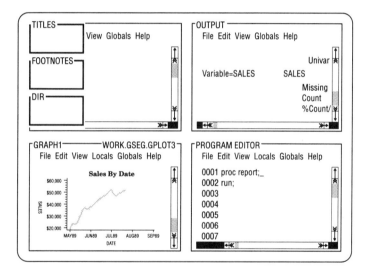

The SAS System offers a useful text editor.

The SAS text editor is a facility available in certain windows of display manager and other windowing environments within the SAS System. You can use the text editor to revise, rearrange or reformat lines of text, check spelling and flag errors, and create and use a spelling dictionary.

What Feature Makes SAS Applications Portable?

The SAS System has a layered MultiVendor Architecture.

Portable applications are possible because the SAS System has a layered structure called MultiVendor Architecture (MVA). Much of the functionality of the SAS System is contained in a portable component, while the host component provides all the required interfaces to the operating system and computer hardware.

Applications reside in the portable component.

Regardless of the differences in hardware and operating system, your SAS applications function the same, look the same, and produce the same results whether you are using a mainframe or a personal computer to process your data.

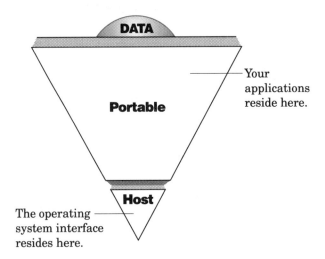

The host component provides all the required interfaces between the SAS System and your operating environment.

The host component of the SAS System is written separately for each environment and allows the SAS System to use the technology provided by individual operating environments. This layered structure means you can use the familiar windows, pull-down menus, and icons available in your host environment to work with SAS applications.

How Do You Benefit from Portable Applications?

You can run the same application in all your computing environments.

Your computing environment is determined by your hardware and the operating system running on it. You can develop SAS applications in one environment and run them in other environments without rewriting.

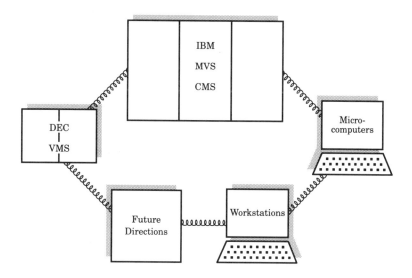

You can take advantage of cooperative processing.

If your site links several types of computers, you can share data and SAS applications across the entire network. The SAS System's exclusive MultiVendor Architecture maintains applications portability while allowing your organization to exploit all the advantages of a particular hardware architecture—from mainframes to workstations and personal computers.

How Does the SAS System Support Applications Development?

The SAS System is a powerful programming language and a collection of ready-to-use programs called procedures.

Combined with other features of the SAS System, the SAS language and its procedures make possible an unlimited variety of applications, from general purpose data processing to highly specialized analyses in diverse application areas. This functionality is surrounded by a sophisticated applications development environment.

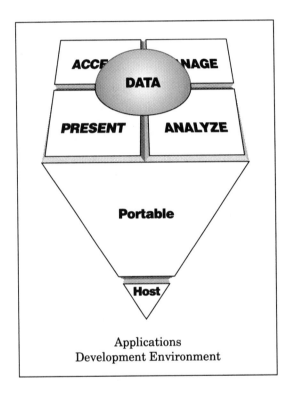

Applications
Development Environment

The SAS System offers tools for creating customized, menu-driven applications.

Applications developers can package complete systems for users, who can then invoke the desired application with a single command. To develop an application, you can write SAS programs and provide a means for running them, often adding some way for the user to interact with the application as it runs. The applications development environment enables you to

- control all the aspects of an interactive program, including building menus, handling errors, controlling program branching, and customizing messages and screens.

- tailor front-end menus and data entry screens for batch and production jobs and submit them from an interactive session.

What Kind of Applications Can You Develop?

The integrated modular design of the SAS System makes an infinite variety of applications possible.

Because the SAS System gives you control of the four data-driven tasks, you can develop applications for any need. All components in the SAS System are integrated so that you can combine and recombine them to handle specific tasks within your organization. The integrated modular design ensures that you can add functionality as your needs change.

The SAS System offers capabilities for every aspect of your business.

A sample of the SAS System's capabilities includes

- ☐ decision support
- ☐ executive information systems
- ☐ financial analysis and reporting
- ☐ market research and sales management
- ☐ project management
- ☐ computer performance evaluation
- ☐ laboratory data analysis
- ☐ quality improvement.

The SAS System offers an applications builder for executive information systems.

Developers can take advantage of the SAS System's applications builder, an interactive facility that links program objects together to form applications. With the applications builder, you can quickly design executive information systems that provide managers essential information for decision making.

Do You Want to Know More about the SAS System?

Explore its capabilities in this book.

This book answers some of the basic questions you may have about the SAS System. The chapters are arranged by functional area. Each chapter shows you a feature that makes the SAS System such an easy-to-use, versatile software system. In the next chapter, you'll learn how to work in the display manager interface using its system of windows and pull-down menus. Then you'll learn ways to access, manage, and present data using a few simple language statements or windows. Finally, you'll see how all these features can be combined into powerful customized applications.

Try some of the examples.

As you read through this book, you'll see that the examples are based on very simple data. This book doesn't provide complete or step-by-step instructions, but it is written so that you can explore features by following the examples.

Go ahead and give it a try. You'll soon see how the SAS System delivers the information and applications you need.

CHAPTER 2

Programming with the SAS® Display Manager System

The programs you see in this book may surprise you. They are short, simple, and straightforward.

SAS programs can serve many purposes. Some merely open windows that enable you to accomplish your task. You can write others that are complex enough to meet any of the data processing needs of your organization. All SAS programs can produce results with a few powerful statements.

In this chapter, you'll find one or two important rules for writing SAS programs. This chapter also introduces you to the windowing environment of the SAS Display Manager System. Using display manager is a quick, convenient, and easy way to start programming because you can submit programs and view the results conveniently on your display.

What Are SAS Programs Like?

SAS programs have DATA steps and PROC steps.

SAS programs consist of one or more steps made up of instructions called statements. The steps are always one of two types: DATA steps or PROC steps. As you'll learn later, the tasks you want to perform determine which type of step you use. This book generally shows examples of PROC steps.

Steps vary in order and length.

For processing, you simply arrange the steps in the order you want tasks to be performed. The SAS System processes the first step, then the second, and so on, independently of other steps. The steps in a SAS program vary in length according to the number of instructions you specify for the task. Here's an example of a one-step program that opens a windowing environment. You'll find an explanation of the statements later in this book.

```
proc fsview data=sasuser.houses;
run;
```

Each step ends with a RUN statement.

It's good programming practice to separate steps in SAS programs with a RUN statement. The following is an example of a program with two PROC steps:

```
1   proc print data=sasuser.houses;
        var street bedrooms baths price;
        where price lt 150000 and bedrooms gt 2;
    run;

2   proc chart data=sasuser.houses;
        vbar price;
    run;
```

1   The first step lists street addresses, number of bedrooms and bathrooms, and prices for houses that sell for less than $150,000 and have more than two bedrooms.

2   The second step displays a vertical bar chart showing the number of houses available in each price range.

What Are the Rules for Writing Statements?

Once again, there are just a few important rules to remember. A SAS statement is an instruction that tells the SAS System to perform some task or gives it some information.

Begin each statement with a keyword.

Most SAS statements begin with a keyword. Keywords tell the SAS System to expect certain instructions or information to follow.

End each statement with a semicolon.

You signal the end of each SAS statement with a semicolon. One of the most common mistakes new users make when starting with the SAS System is forgetting the semicolon.

Separate elements within statements by blanks and sometimes by special characters.

You separate elements within statements with one or more blanks. The number doesn't matter. Some elements are separated by special characters, depending on the requirements of the statement.

You can see that this sentence-like structure allows you flexibility. You can write statements

☐　in uppercase, lowercase, or a mixture of the two

☐　over more than one line

☐　with more than one statement on a line.

All of the following are acceptable ways to write the same SAS statement:

```
class STYLE BEDROOMS;

class
    style
    bedrooms;

class style bedrooms; var price;
```

This book always shows examples in all lowercase letters, except for the text of labels and titles. Statements are on one line where space permits.

How Do You Start the SAS System?

Select the display manager interface.

The first step to SAS programming is starting the SAS System with the display manager interface. When you work with display manager, all the activities you perform from the time you start the SAS System until you stop it are called your SAS session. You can control and view all the parts of your SAS session from display manager windows.

Start a SAS session with the SAS command.

You start your SAS session by issuing the SAS command at the operating system prompt. On personal computers and in some computing environments, you automatically start display manager when you specify this command:

```
sas
```

In other computing environments, you need to request display manager as you start your session by specifying the DMS option after the command. Other sites may use a customized form of the SAS command or allow you to start your SAS session from a logon menu. If you don't have instructions for starting the SAS System in display manager mode, ask your SAS Software Consultant for them.

What Happens First after You Start Display Manager?

The LOG window and PROGRAM EDITOR window appear when you start your SAS session.

As the SAS session starts, you'll see a display with two windows. Both windows have a command line in the upper left corner and a text area beneath.

Look for messages in the LOG window.

The window at the top of your display is the LOG window. The program statements you submit and any messages from the SAS System about your SAS session are displayed here.

Type and submit programs from the PROGRAM EDITOR window.

You type your SAS programs into the text area of the PROGRAM EDITOR window, which is at the bottom of your initial display. The PROGRAM EDITOR window is marked with numbered lines where you can use the full-screen capabilities of the SAS text editor.

```
┌LOG────────────────────────────────────────────────────────┐
│  Command ===>                                              │
│                                                            │
│                                                            │
│                                                            │
│                                                            │
│                                                            │
│                                                            │
│                                                            │
│                                                            │
│                                                            │
│                                                            │
└────────────────────────────────────────────────────────────┘
┌PROGRAM EDITOR──────────────────────────────────────────────┐
│  Command ===>                                              │
│                                                            │
│  00001                                                     │
│  00002                                                     │
│  00003                                                     │
│  00004                                                     │
│  00005                                                     │
│  00006                                                     │
│  00007                                                     │
│  00008                                                     │
│  00009                                                     │
└────────────────────────────────────────────────────────────┘
```

How Do You Control the Environment?

Once you start working, you can move from one window to another, submit programs, and ask for online help. Display manager commands, function keys, and pull-down menus enable you to control and modify your SAS session.

Issue commands from the command line.

Display manager commands are instructions you type on the command line. You issue the command by pressing the ENTER or RETURN key.

Press function keys.

Many common display manager commands are assigned to function keys. If you issue the KEYS command from any window, you get a KEYS window that tells you which function key definitions are active. The following illustration shows you the default key settings for a sample display manager session.

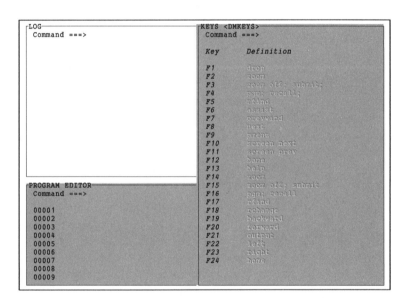

Are Menus Available in Display Manager?

Activate the PMENU facility.

You can also control your SAS session with pull-down menus provided by the PMENU facility of the SAS System. The pull-down menus work well with a mouse attachment, but you can also use your keyboard to select items. Issue the PMENU command to replace the command line with an action bar.

Select items from the action bar, then select items from pull-down menus.

When you select an item from the action bar, the SAS System displays a pull-down menu of tasks you can perform. The following display shows you the options available on the Globals pull-down menu.

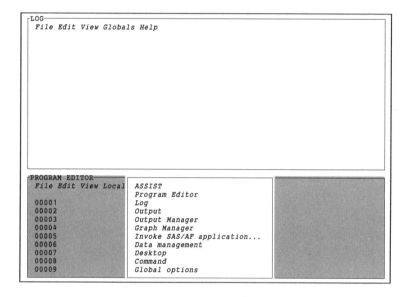

How Do You Run SAS Programs?

Type the statements into the PROGRAM EDITOR window.

This section shows you how to prepare and submit a typical SAS program. The example introduces a deliberate error to show you a typical message in the LOG window and to show you how to recall programs. Here, the VAR statement is missing a semicolon.

```
title 'Houses for Less Than $150,000';

proc print data=sasuser.houses;
    var street bedrooms baths price
    where price lt 150000 and bedrooms gt 2;
run;
```

Submit the program using the pull-down menus.

The statements you type in the PROGRAM EDITOR window won't perform any action until you submit them as a program to the SAS System. To run the program, select **Submit** from the Locals pull-down menu. Before you press the ENTER or RETURN key, your display should look like this.

```
┌LOG──────────────────────────────────────────────────────────────┐
│  File Edit View Globals Help                                      │
│                                                                   │
│                                                                   │
│                                                                   │
│                                                                   │
│                                                                   │
│                                                                   │
│                                                                   │
│                                                                   │
│                                                                   │
│                                                                   │
├PROGRAM EDITOR─────────────────────────────────────────────────── │
│  File Edit View │Locals│ Globals Help                             │
│                 ┌──────────────────────┐                         │
│  00001 title '  │ Submit               │ 50,000';                 │
│  00002          │ Recall text          │                         │
│  00003 proc pr  │ Submit top line...   │ ;                        │
│  00004    var   │ Signon...            │ rice                     │
│  00005    wher  │ Remote submit        │ edrooms gt 2;            │
│  00006 run;     │ Signoff...           │                          │
│  00007          └──────────────────────┘                         │
│  00008                                                            │
│  00009                                                            │
└──────────────────────────────────────────────────────────────────┘
```

What Happens if There's An Error?

Look for messages in the LOG window.

You receive information about errors in the LOG window. Errors are underlined or explained with a message or both.

Because the error in this program is a missing semicolon, the message refers to the keyword in the next statement. The SAS System didn't recognize the end of the VAR statement and tried to read the keyword WHERE as one of the list of variables.

```
┌LOG────────────────────────────────────────────────────────────────┐
│ File Edit View Globals Help                                        │
│                                                                    │
│  1     title 'Houses for Less Than $150,000';                      │
│  2                                                                 │
│  3     proc print data=sasuser.houses;                             │
│  4        var street bedrooms baths price                          │
│  5        where price lt 150000 and bedrooms gt 2;                 │
│                   ------                    -                       │
│                   200                       200                     │
│  ERROR: Variable WHERE not found.                                  │
│  6     run;                                                        │
│                                                                    │
│  ERROR 200-322: The symbol is not recognized.                      │
│                                                                    │
│  NOTE: The SAS System stopped processing this step because of errors. │
│  NOTE: The PROCEDURE PRINT used 0.02 CPU seconds and 1585K.        │
│                                                                    │
├PROGRAM EDITOR──────────────────────────────────────────────────────┤
│ File Edit View Locals Globals Help                                 │
│ NOTE: 6 Lines submitted.                                           │
│ 00001                                                              │
│ 00002                                                              │
│ 00003                                                              │
│ 00004                                                              │
│ 00005                                                              │
│ 00006                                                              │
│ 00007                                                              │
│ 00008                                                              │
│ 00009                                                              │
└────────────────────────────────────────────────────────────────────┘
```

Recall programs you have submitted.

You can correct your program easily. Each time you submit statements, they are stored in sequence in a recall buffer. To copy them back into the PROGRAM EDITOR window, select **Recall text** from the Locals pull-down menu. Type a semicolon at the end of the VAR statement to make your program look like this:

```
title 'Houses for Less Than $150,000';

proc print data=sasuser.houses;
    var street bedrooms baths price;
    where price lt 150000 and bedrooms gt 2;
run;
```

Where Are Results Displayed?

Look for results in the OUTPUT window.

To run your corrected program, submit the program again. As soon as the results are ready, display manager automatically displays them in the OUTPUT window.

```
┌OUTPUT──────────────────────────────────────PROC PRINT suspended─┐
│ File Edit View Globals Help                                      │
│                    Houses for Less Than $150,000               1 │
│                                                                  │
│          OBS    STREET            BEDROOMS   BATHS      PRICE     │
│                                                                  │
│           4     Garris Street        4        3.0     $107,250   │
│           5     Kemble Avenue        3        3.0      $86,650    │
│           6     West Drive           4        3.0      $94,450    │
│           7     Graham Avenue        3        1.5      $73,650    │
│           8     Hampshire Avenue     3        2.5      $79,350    │
│          10     Jeans Avenue         4        2.5     $127,150    │
│          11     State Highway        3        3.0      $89,100    │
│          14     Highland Road        4        2.5     $102,950    │
│                                                                  │
└──────────────────────────────────────────────────────────────────┘
```

If you have more than one page of results, you can scroll through the pages with pull-down menus, function keys, or commands.

```
┌OUTPUT─────────────────────────────────────────────────────────┐
│ File Edit View Globals Help                                    │
│                 Number of Houses in Each Price Range         2 │
│                                                                │
│  Frequency                                                     │
│   5 +                            *****                         │
│     |                            *****                         │
│   4 +                    *****   *****                         │
│     |                    *****   *****                         │
│   3 +                    *****   *****   *****                 │
│     |                    *****   *****   *****                 │
│   2 +                    *****   *****   *****   *****          │
│     |                    *****   *****   *****   *****          │
│   1 +    *****   *****   *****   *****   *****                  │
│     |    *****   *****   *****   *****   *****                  │
│     ------------------------------------------------------     │
│          $40,000  $60,000  $80,000  $100,000  $120,000         │
│                          Asking price                          │
└────────────────────────────────────────────────────────────────┘
```

Can You Manage the Results?

You can edit, print, or file the results of your program from the OUTPUT MANAGER window.

The OUTPUT MANAGER window lists the results from each program you submit and provides some information about them. If you run several programs during your session, the output for each one is numbered and stored in sequence for the duration of your SAS session.

```
┌OUTPUT MANAGER────────────────────────────────────────────────────────
  Edit View Globals Help

      Procedure  Page#   Pages        Description
   _  PRINT         1      1           Houses for Less Than $150,000
   _  CHART         2      1           Number of Houses in Each Price Range
```

Other windows make your work easier to manage.

You can customize the size, shape, placement, and colors of each window in display manager. In addition to the three initial windows, display manager offers windows that help you manage your SAS files. There are also desktop aids such as the NOTEPAD, CALCULATOR, and APPOINTMENT windows.

How Do You End a SAS Session?

Save any programs or output you want to keep.

When you end your SAS session, the SAS System deletes all the messages and output stored in the LOG and OUTPUT windows. It also deletes all the programs stored in the recall buffer. If you want to save your output or programs, you must save them in a permanent file. Select **Save as** from the File pull-down menu. The SAS System will prompt you for an appropriate filename.

The filename will, of course, depend on your operating system. Under the MVS operating system, you can store the program in a member of a partitioned data set. Under CMS, you store your programs in a CMS file with the filetype SAS. Under directory-based systems, you generally add the extension .SAS to programs you want to store and run again.

Exit the SAS System.

Once you have saved your programs and results, you can end your SAS session by selecting **Exit** from the File pull-down menu.

```
┌LOG────────────────────────────────────────────────────────────┐
│   File Edit View Globals Help                                  │
│                                                                │
│                                                                │
│                                                                │
│                                                                │
│                                                                │
│                                                                │
│                                                                │
│                                                                │
│                                                                │
│                                                                │
│                                                                │
┌PROGRAM EDITOR──────────────────────────────────────────────────┐
│   File Edit View Locals Globals Help                           │
│  ┌──────────┐                                                  │
│  │ Open     │                                                  │
│  │ Save     │                                                  │
│  │ Save as  │                                                  │
│  │ Print    │                                                  │
│  │ Exit...  │                                                  │
│  └──────────┘                                                  │
│   00007                                                        │
│   00008                                                        │
│   00009                                                        │
└────────────────────────────────────────────────────────────────┘
```

C H A P T E R   3
Accessing Data

Today's large data bases, while giving you massive amounts of data storage, have also created islands of data throughout your organization. Data are accessible to some departments but not to others. The SAS System gives you greater control over data access by providing direct and transparent interfaces between your applications and your data no matter where they are stored. The SAS System provides a means for reading data that are

☐   ready for data entry

☐   stored in files formatted by other software products, such as database management software

☐   stored in other file formats.

This chapter describes the features of SAS data sets and gives you an overview of the ways to access your data.

What Types of Data Can the SAS System Access?

Data that are ready for data entry.

If you are a new user, the windowing interfaces of the FSEDIT and FSVIEW procedures provide a convenient method for data entry, editing, and retrieval. If you are developing applications for others, the FSEDIT and FSVIEW procedures are the basis of more sophisticated data entry and data presentation systems. Each procedure provides tools for customizing windows, defining the characteristics of your data entry fields, and performing cross-validation of field values and other data manipulations.

Data that are stored in database management systems.

The SAS System can transparently access the data in many popular database management systems such as IBM Corporation's DB2, Digital Equipment Corporation's Rdb/VMS, and Oracle Corporation's ORACLE. This capability is possible because of two features of the SAS System: SAS data sets and engines. The SAS System can process any data that it recognizes as a SAS data set. Engines are parts of the SAS System that read data stored in various formats and present them for processing in the form of a SAS data set.

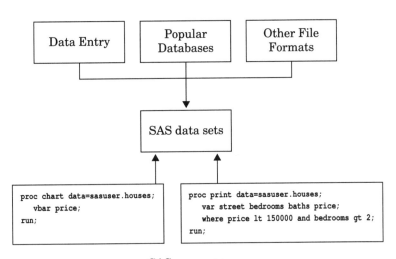

SAS programs

Data that are stored in other file formats.

One of the most powerful features of the SAS language is its ability to read almost any file format, including hierarchical files, variable-length fields and records, and multiple records. Statements in the SAS language allow you to describe complex record layouts and control how they are output.

What Are SAS Data Sets?

To start, you may want to look at the structure of a SAS data set. It may or may not differ from other files you work with, such as two-dimensional spreadsheets or some database software products.

SAS data sets have variables and observations.

In SAS data sets, the data values are arranged in a rectangular, tablelike structure. The columns of the table are called variables. Variables compare with fields or cells in other types of files. The rows are called observations. Observations are equivalent to records.

SAS data sets contain descriptor information.

Another identifying feature is the descriptor information contained in each SAS data set. During processing, the SAS System reads the descriptor information to determine the attributes of the data set and the number and characteristics of each variable.

In summary, all SAS data sets represent a set of data values and the descriptor information. This common structure means that all SAS programs recognize the data, so you don't have to supply information about the data sets and data in your SAS programs.

Where Are SAS Data Sets Stored?

SAS data sets are stored in SAS data libraries.

SAS data sets are stored in collections of files called SAS data libraries. SAS data sets are the most commonly used type of SAS file, but a SAS data library can contain other types of SAS files. These collections enable the SAS System to locate your files and refer to them in your SAS programs.

SAS data libraries have different representations on each host operating system.

SAS data libraries have different representations and naming conventions on each host operating system. They are roughly equivalent to the level of file organization on your host operating system.

On This Host Operating System	Your SAS Data Library Organized As
directory-based	directory
MVS	specially formatted operating system data set
CMS	minidisk (file mode)

SAS data libraries are identified by librefs.

No matter which host operating system you use, you identify SAS data libraries by assigning each one a libref. Librefs are temporary, shorthand ways of referring to SAS data libraries in your program statements. You must assign them each time you start a SAS session. Generally, you submit a LIBNAME statement to associate the libref you choose with the host operating system name for the library.

```
libname mylib 'SAS-data-library';
```

The SAS System provides two SAS data libraries.

The SAS System automatically assigns at least two librefs every time you start a new SAS session.

SASUSER
> refers to a permanent library where your SAS data sets are kept for use the next time you work with the SAS System. This book shows you how to store your practice files here for convenience.

WORK
> refers to a temporary library. Useful for developing and testing new programs, the files in the WORK library are deleted at the end of each session.

How Do You Refer to SAS Data Sets?

Assign a libref.

If you are creating a permanent SAS data set or accessing an existing one, the first thing you must do is identify the SAS data library. At the beginning of your SAS session, assign a libref to the libraries you plan to read from and write to. The only exceptions are the SASUSER library used in this book and the temporary WORK library. The SAS System assigns these automatically.

Name the SAS data set.

You name SAS data sets when you create them. This name is stored as part of the descriptor information for the data set. When naming SAS data sets, you must remember a few rules.

Valid Name	Not Valid	Reason
seedwt	seedweight	more than 8 characters or numbers
data_84	data/84	contains special symbol
ex07r532	07ex532r	begins with number
_84_data	84data	begins with number

Use a two-part name for permanent SAS data sets.

The names of all permanent SAS data sets have two parts separated by a period: the libref you assign for the session and the name of the data set.

librefs <   > data set names

For data sets in the temporary library, you can use just the data set name; that is, you can omit the libref WORK. The SAS System looks for those data sets in the WORK library and deletes them at the end of your SAS session.

How Do You Create a New Data Set?

Try interactive data entry with the FSEDIT procedure.

For data that aren't already stored on the computer, you can enter your data directly into a SAS data set. The FSEDIT procedure is a convenient and easy-to-learn windowing environment. With the FSEDIT procedure, you can name your data set, describe its variables, and enter observations one at a time into a data entry window.

Name the SAS data set.

To name the new SAS data set REGIONS and open the window for the FSEDIT procedure, submit the following program:

```
proc fsedit new=sasuser.regions;
run;
```

Describe the variables in the FSEDIT New window.

You describe the variables in the FSEDIT New window. All windows in the FSEDIT procedure have a command line and areas for entering text. Before you start filling in the fields, you should understand what information is requested.

```
┌FSEDIT New SASUSER.REGIONS──────────────────────────────────
│ View Locals Globals Help
│
│ Name    Type Length              Label              Format
```

What Is an Example?

These are the raw data.

You can easily describe the following raw data to the SAS System using the FSEDIT New window.

mountain	*12389.46*	*10jan90*	*general*	*fee*
coastal	*1000.00*	*06may89*	*research*	*gift*
coastal	*9337.67*	*02jan90*	*general*	*fee*
university	*10005.15*	*04jan90*	*general*	*fee*
metro	*500.00*			*gift*
metro	*21296.47*	*04jan90*	*general*	*fee*
metro	*5000.00*	*15jul90*	*research*	*gift*

You can simply name each variable, and the SAS System will supply default values for the other attributes. To gain more control over how the data are read, stored, and displayed, you'll want to assign attributes.

These are the attributes assigned to SAS variables.

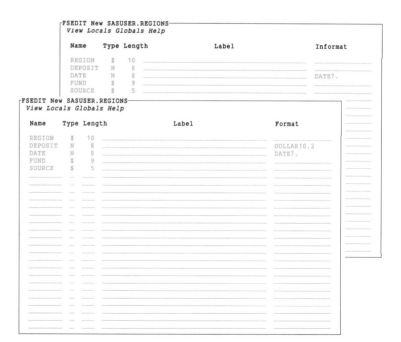

The pages that follow describe in more detail some of the attributes you can assign to your SAS variables.

How Do You Describe Variables?

Name the variables.

To describe variables, supply the requested information in the FSEDIT New window. Only the variable name is required. The SAS System supplies default values for the other attributes, and you can leave them blank if you want.

Specify the type.

SAS variables are either numeric or character. You indicate a numeric variable by leaving the field blank or by specifying an N. Indicate character variables with a C or a $ (dollar sign).

Assign a length for storage.

The length you specify is the number of bytes the variable occupies in storage. The SAS System will assign a default length of 8 bytes to numeric and character variables if you are using the FSEDIT procedure. If your character variables are longer or shorter, specify the length of the longest value, allowing 1 byte per character.

Supply a label if you like.

You can provide your own headings for report columns by specifying a permanent label for each variable. Labels can be longer than the 8 characters allowed for variable names, and they can contain blanks, national characters, and special symbols.

Examples of Labels

```
Personnel Available on July 3, 1989
März
Input/Output Ratio
```

Can the SAS System Handle Dates and Other Special Values?

The SAS System provides templates for reading and writing dates and other special values.

Dates are numeric variables in the SAS System, and they are stored as the number of days before or after January 1, 1960. To store and display dates correctly, you must supply templates that tell the SAS System how to read dates and how to display them. These templates are called informats and formats. The SAS System provides a number of them not only for reading date values but also for money values and other forms of data.

Specify an informat to read the date.

Informats tell the SAS System how to read character or numeric values. Each informat includes the length of the value you want to read. Don't forget the period—it's part of the informat. The following table shows common date and U. S. currency informats and the raw data values they can read.

Informat	Value Read	Value Stored
mmddyy8.	01/25/48	− 4359
date7.	07Jul90	11145
comma7.	$3,452.50	3452.5

Specify a format to display the date.

To display special values such as dates, you must specify a format. Otherwise, the SAS System displays the values stored in the data set. As part of the format, you can specify the length of the value you want to display. The following table shows two common date and a U. S. currency format and the form in which the data are displayed.

Format	Value Stored	Value Displayed
date7.	− 4359	25JAN48
mmddyy8.	11145	07/07/90
dollar10.2	3452.5	$3,452.50

How Do You Supply Data Values?

Create a SAS data set.

When you've finished describing the variables in the FSEDIT New window, you create an empty SAS data set by selecting **End** from the View pull-down menu.

Go to the FSEDIT window.

The SAS System automatically takes you to the FSEDIT window, where you can start your interactive data entry.

```
┌FSEDIT SASUSER.REGIONS─────────────────────────────────────────Obs 0─┐
│  Edit Search View Locals Globals Help                                │
│  WARNING: No observations on data set.  Please enter END or ADD.      │
│                                                                      │
│                                                                      │
│                                                                      │
│                                                                      │
│                                                                      │
│                              REGION:   _____                    │
│                                                                      │
│                              DEPOSIT:  _____                    │
│                                                                      │
│                              DATE:     _____                      │
│                                                                      │
│                              FUND:     _____                    │
│                                                                      │
│                              SOURCE:   _____                        │
│                                                                      │
│                                                                      │
│                                                                      │
│                                                                      │
│                                                                      │
└──────────────────────────────────────────────────────────────────────┘
```

Enter values for each observation.

To enter the first observation, select **Add new record** from the Edit pull-down menu. Fill in the fields with the data. To enter the next observation, select **Add new record** again and fill in the fields.

Check data values, if you want.

To view the data you've just entered, you can select a number of items from the View pull-down menu that enable you to move easily from observation to observation. The Search pull-down menu lets you look for observations that contain specific values.

Save the SAS data set.

If the data are as you want them, save the finished data set by selecting **End** from the Edit pull-down menu. You're ready to start your analysis and reporting.

What If Your Data Are in a Database?

Access them through SAS data views.

You can access data stored in databases by creating a form of SAS data set known as a SAS data view. A view is a SAS data set that stores only the information that tells the SAS System how to retrieve data values from your database and present them to the SAS System as observations and variables. The view also provides descriptor information.

Create views in a two-stage process.

The windows of the SAS/ACCESS software enable you to create views. There is a SAS/ACCESS interface for most popular data bases.

Stage	Your Task	What You Create
1	Describe the database table to the SAS System	Access descriptor
2	Create one or more view descriptors from the access descriptor	View

Process the view in a DATA step or PROC step.

To process each view, specify its name as input for a DATA step or PROC step as you would specify any other SAS data set. With this capability, you can continue to access and store your data with the database software and still use all the analysis and presentation power available through the SAS System.

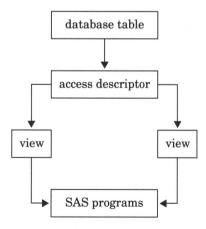

How Do You Create an Access Descriptor?

Start the ACCESS procedure.

To begin, open the ACCESS window by submitting the following PROC step. The ACCESS window lists all the files available during your current SAS session.

```
proc access;
run;
```

Name the access descriptor.

Name the access descriptor by selecting **New** from the File pull-down menu in the ACCESS window. PROC ACCESS prompts you for the libref and name for the access descriptor. The following example names an access descriptor in the temporary SAS data library WORK.

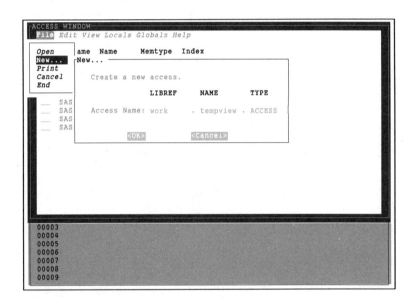

Select an engine, if necessary.

If you have more than one SAS/ACCESS interface product installed at your site, you will be asked to select an engine from the Engine Selection window. The engines are identified by the name of the database each accesses.

How Do You Describe the Database Table?

Identify the table in the Access Descriptor Identification window.

Describe the contents of the table in the Access Descriptor Display window.

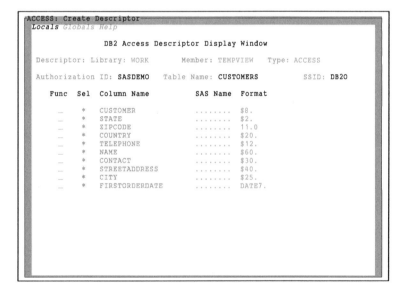

What Are the Steps in Defining a View?

Select an access descriptor from the Access window.

When you save the access descriptor, the SAS System returns you to the Access window. Find the name of the access descriptor, and type CV for Create View in the field to the left of the name. Press the ENTER key to display the View Descriptor Display window.

Name the view, and describe the variables in the View Descriptor window.

You'll see the list of variables you saved in the access descriptor. To select the variables you want included in the view, type an S in the Func column. To change labels, informats, or formats, type over the information shown on the display.

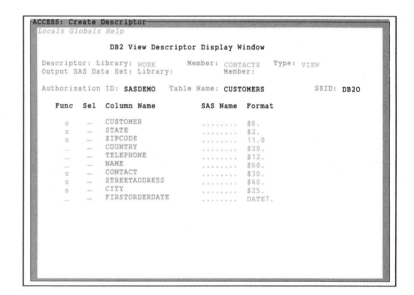

Use the view in your SAS programs.

Save your view by repeatedly selecting **End** from the File pull-down menu. You can now specify your view as input to any SAS program. Just supply the view name as you would the name of any other SAS data set.

```
proc print data=contacts;
run;
```

What If the Data Are Stored in Other Computer Files?

DATA step programs can read any file format that can be described.

Another way to get your data into SAS data sets is through the statements provided by the DATA step. The DATA step is one of the more powerful features of the SAS System because it incorporates a high-level programming language with a data management facility.

You submit SAS statements to accomplish the basic tasks.

When entering data interactively or creating a view of some data, you use windowing facilities to accomplish tasks. With the DATA step you must use the statements of the DATA step to

☐ name the SAS data set you want to create

☐ identify the file you want to read

☐ describe how to read the data fields from each record in the file.

For simple data, the statements are straightforward. For more complex data formats, the SAS System provides statements that enable you to read in a wide variety of formats, including hierarchical files, variable-length fields and records, and multiple records.

What Are the Parts of a DATA Step?

The raw data files look like this.   Recall the data you entered interactively with the FSEDIT procedure.

```
mountain     12389.46   10jan90   general    fee
coastal       1000.00   06may89   research   gift
coastal       9337.67   02jan90   general    fee
university   10005.15   04jan90   general    fee
metro         500.00                          gift
metro        21296.47   04jan90   general    fee
metro        5000.00    15jul90   research   gift
```

The DATA step looks like this.   If the data were already stored in the format shown above, you could just as easily have submitted the following program to create a SAS data set.

```
1 libname mylib 'SAS-data-library';

2 data mylib.regional;
3     infile 'your-input-file';
4     input region $ 1-10 deposit 12-20
            @ 22 date date07. fund $ 30-38
            source $ 40-44;
5 run;
```

Here's what each statement does.

1   The LIBNAME statement identifies where you want the SAS System to store any permanent SAS data sets you create.

2   The DATA statement tells the SAS System to create a new data set and supply its name in a DATA statement.

3   The INFILE statement specifies the name of the raw data file where the data are stored.

4   The INPUT statement names each variable, specifies its type, and identifies the columns where the values are located in the raw data file.

5   The RUN statement ends the DATA step.

C H A P T E R   4

Managing Data

When working with large quantities of data, you probably spend much of your computer time and resources managing those data. The SAS System has many features that you can use to group, edit, rearrange, and combine your data.

This chapter shows you how to use two of those features, the FSVIEW procedure and the SQL procedure, to edit values and perform two ad hoc queries of a simple SAS data set.

How Do You Browse Data Values?

You can browse data in table form or one observation at a time.

As you saw in the previous chapter, once you enter data values with the FSEDIT procedure, you can scroll through the data set one observation at a time. To display observations and variables as rows and columns, use the FSVIEW procedure.

Use the FSVIEW procedure to view data in table form.

Submit the following program to browse the SAS data set SASUSER.REGIONS.

```
proc fsview data=sasuser.regions;
run;
```

Missing values appear as periods or blanks.

Note that SASUSER.REGIONS contains missing values for the variables DATE and FUND. The SAS System represents missing values for character variables with a blank. Missing values of numeric variables are represented with a period.

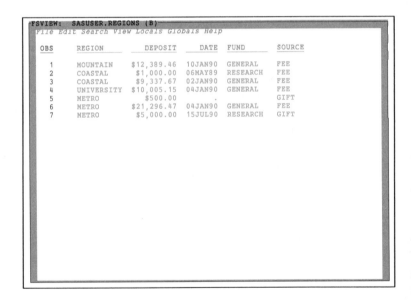

```
FSVIEW:   SASUSER.REGIONS (B)
  File Edit Search View Locals Globals Help

  OBS      REGION       DEPOSIT     DATE   FUND        SOURCE

   1       MOUNTAIN    $12,389.46  10JAN90 GENERAL     FEE
   2       COASTAL      $1,000.00  06MAY89 RESEARCH    FEE
   3       COASTAL      $9,337.67  02JAN90 GENERAL     FEE
   4       UNIVERSITY  $10,005.15  04JAN90 GENERAL     FEE
   5       METRO          $500.00       .              GIFT
   6       METRO       $21,296.47  04JAN90 GENERAL     FEE
   7       METRO        $5,000.00  15JUL90 RESEARCH    GIFT
```

How Do You Modify Data Values?

Open the data set for editing.

You can submit the following statements to open the SAS data set for editing:

```
proc fsview data=sasuser.regions edit;
run;
```

Specify whether you want to modify one observation at a time or all observations.

By default, the SAS System opens the data set so that you can edit only one record at a time. This feature enables other users to edit the same data set at the same time. To modify an observation, move your cursor anywhere on that line and press the ENTER or RETURN key. When the observation is highlighted, you can type the new information in the field. If you want to make several changes, you can make all observations available for editing by requesting MEMBER modification mode. Select **Set modification mode** from the Edit pull-down menu.

Move to the field and change the value.

In this example, you want to add the missing values. In the fifth observation, type the value 05JUN89 for the variable DATE and the value EDUCATION for the variable FUND.

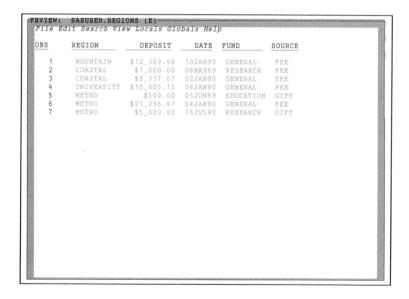

How Can You Sort Data Values?

Specify the variable or variables you want to sort by.

The SAS System can sort observations by the values of one or more character or numeric variables. Select **Sort** from the View pull-down menu, and specify the variable REGION.

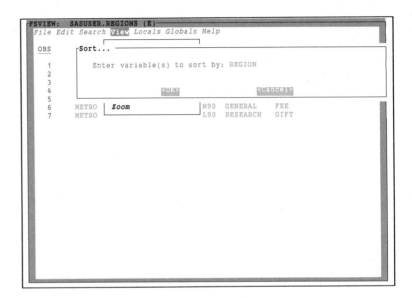

After sorting, observations are displayed and stored in sorted order.

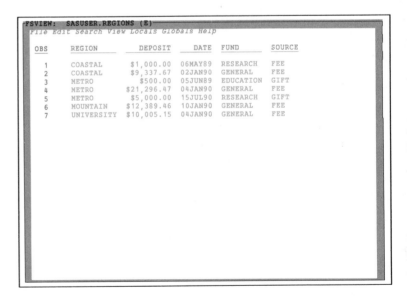

How Do You Select Observations for Display?

Subset the data with a WHERE expression.

A WHERE expression is an arithmetic or logical expression written with SAS operators and one or more numeric or character variables. You can use comparison and arithmetic operators to compare the values of a variable to a constant or to the value of another variable. Logical operators such as OR and AND enable you to combine expressions.

Examples of WHERE Expressions

```
where date > '01JAN87'd and region='METRO'
where idnum is missing
where taxes gt salary*.333
```

To select observations based on the values of the variable FUND, select **Where** from the Search pull-down menu and type the following WHERE expression:

```
fund='GENERAL'
```

Remember to write character values in the correct case and enclose them in single quotes.

Only the observations that satisfy the WHERE expression are displayed.

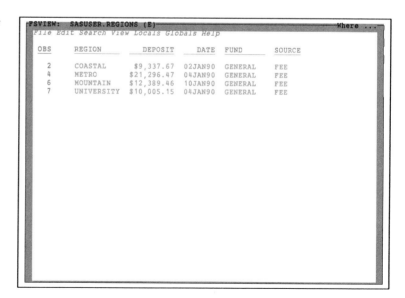

How Do You Select Variables for Display?

You can show, drop, or move variables.

To drop the variables DATE, FUND, and SOURCE from this example, select **Arrange variables** from the View pull-down menu.

Select the variables you want to drop.

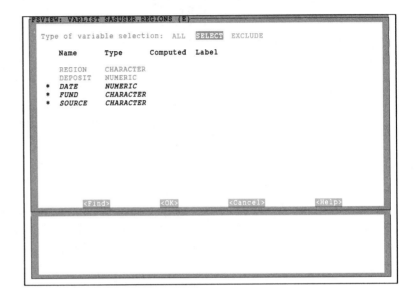

Only the variables you want to show are displayed.

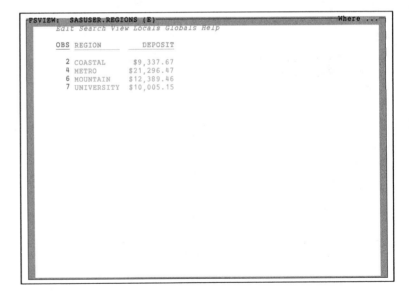

How Do You Calculate New Variables?

Name and define a formula for the new variable.

You can calculate new variables from existing variables by defining formulas. To create the new variable, select **Define formula** from the Locals pull-down menu.

Specify variable attributes and formulas in the Define command window.

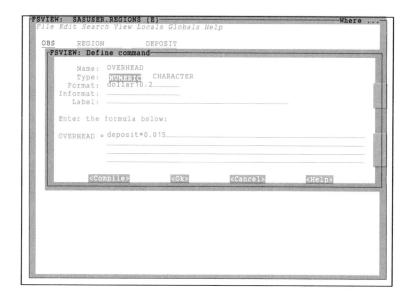

Display the values of the new variable.

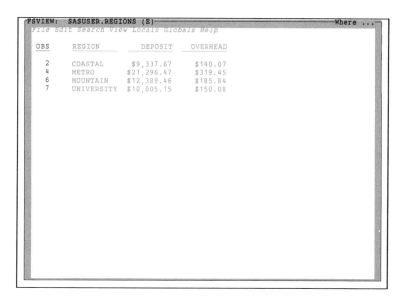

What If You Want to Store the Results?

Name the new data set.

Once you subset the data and calculate the values of new variables, you can store a new SAS data set containing only the variables and observations that appear on your display. Select **Save as** from the File pull-down menu. For this example, store the subset as SASUSER.OVERHEAD and indicate that you do not want to select all variables.

Select the variables.

The VARLIST window of the FSVIEW procedure prompts you for the variables you want to store in the data set. You can indicate that you want to save all the variables, or you can select variables from the list.

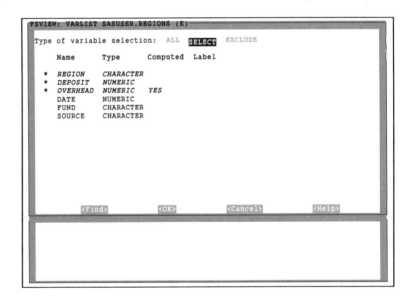

Save the new data set and continue editing.

After you save the data set SASUSER.OVERHEAD, the FSVIEW procedure is still active. The data in SASUSER.REGIONS remain unchanged, and you can continue to subset, modify, and calculate new values.

What Other Features Are Available for Queries?

You can choose the DATA step or the SQL procedure.

Statements in the DATA step enable you to

☐ perform ad hoc queries

☐ add or modify variables

☐ select subsets of your data

☐ create new SAS data sets.

If you are familiar with Structured Query Language (SQL), the SAS System implements this widely used query language through the SQL procedure. The SQL procedure processes SQL statements that read and update SAS data sets. Its capabilities complement the powerful DATA step as a tool for data management.

You can work with data from many sources.

For example, you can use the SQL procedure to combine variables from many different sources including more than one SAS data set, views created by SAS/ACCESS software, or a combination of these sources.

Once you start the SQL procedure, you can perform as many SQL activities as you want. When you finish, you can submit other SAS statements or issue the QUIT statement to stop the SQL procedure.

You can use analogous statements.

As you read SQL programs, you'll want to remember the following analogies between SAS terminology and SQL terminology.

SQL Procedure	SAS System	Other Software
table or view	SAS data set	file
row	observation	record
column	variable	field

What's an Example of an SQL Query?

Start the SQL procedure.

Submit the following program statement to start the procedure. You don't need to specify a data set name because you can work with more than one during this session.

```
proc sql;
```

Browse a data set and create new variables.

This example shows the PROC SQL statements that select the variables REGION and DEPOSIT and create a new variable, OPERCOST. These actions are limited to observations for which the value of FUND is GENERAL.

```
select region, deposit,
       deposit*.015 as opercost format=dollar10.2
    from sasuser.regions
    where fund='GENERAL';
```

View the results.

Results are displayed for you automatically when you use the SQL procedure to subset data.

```
                    The SAS System                      1

        REGION        DEPOSIT    OPERCOST
        ------------------------------------------
        COASTAL       $9,337.67   $140.07
        METRO        $21,296.47   $319.45
        MOUNTAIN     $12,389.46   $185.84
        UNIVERSITY   $10,005.15   $150.08
```

Does the SQL Procedure Create SAS Data Sets?

Store the data or the SQL query.
Once you have created new variables, combined portions of SAS data sets, or subset larger SAS data sets, you can store the data or the SQL statements you used to create them. Submit the following statements to store the data as a SAS data set:

```
create table sasuser.opercost as
select region, deposit,
      deposit*.015 as opercost format=dollar10.2
    from sasuser.regions
    where fund='GENERAL';
```

Stop the SQL procedure.
You can stop the SQL procedure by submitting a DATA step or another PROC step. Submitting a QUIT statement also ends your SQL session.

```
quit;
```

CHAPTER 5

Presenting Data in Reports

Once you have collected and prepared your data, you can report the results in ways that clearly communicate the significance of your findings.

SAS procedures often display results in report form; however, the SAS System also provides a number of procedures especially for producing reports. This chapter shows you a simple detail report and a summary report.

What Is the Simplest Report I Can Write?

Detail reports are lists of data values.

Detail reports are easy with the SAS System. You can use the PRINT procedure to list all the values in a SAS data set. Each observation is identified with an observation number, and all the variables have headers that identify the contents of the columns. The SAS System adds a default title at the top of each report.

To obtain a detail report of the SAS data set SASUSER.REGIONS used throughout this book, submit the following PROC step:

```
proc print data=sasuser.regions;
run;
```

The simplest report contains variable names, observation numbers, and a default title.

```
                              The SAS System                                1

    OBS    REGION        DEPOSIT        DATE      FUND        SOURCE

      1    COASTAL      $1,000.00     06MAY89    RESEARCH     FEE
      2    COASTAL      $9,337.67     02JAN90    GENERAL      FEE
      3    METRO          $500.00     05JUN89    EDUCATION    GIFT
      4    METRO       $21,296.47     04JAN90    GENERAL      FEE
      5    METRO        $5,000.00     15JUL90    RESEARCH     GIFT
      6    MOUNTAIN    $12,389.46     10JAN90    GENERAL      FEE
      7    UNIVERSITY  $10,005.15     04JAN90    GENERAL      FEE
```

Can You Control Which Columns Print?

You can specify variables and their order.

A VAR statement is available for the PRINT procedure. To select the variables for your report, list the variable names in the order you want them to appear in the columns of your report. For example, the following statements select variables for the detail report on SASUSER.REGIONS:

```
var region source deposit;
```

You can request observation numbers not be printed.

The SAS System provides observation numbers by default. If you don't want to print them, add the NOOBS option to the PROC PRINT statement. The following program produces a detail report with the columns you selected:

```
proc print data=sasuser.regions noobs;
   var region source deposit;
run;
```

```
                            The SAS System                              1

                    REGION        SOURCE        DEPOSIT

                    COASTAL       FEE           $1,000.00
                    COASTAL       FEE           $9,337.67
                    METRO         GIFT            $500.00
                    METRO         FEE          $21,296.47
                    METRO         GIFT          $5,000.00
                    MOUNTAIN      FEE          $12,389.46
                    UNIVERSITY    FEE          $10,005.15
```

What Features Enhance the Appearance of the List?

You can request descriptive labels.

Each time you print a report, you can add temporary labels to your variables with the LABEL statement. For the PRINT procedure, you must also add the LABEL option to the PROC PRINT statement to tell it to use the temporary labels in printing the report.

You can add titles.

The TITLE statement enables you to specify a 40-character title for your SAS output. You can assign more than one label with successive title statements such as TITLE1, TITLE2 and so forth. These titles remain in effect throughout your SAS session.

The following PROC PRINT step produces a table with descriptive labels and a title:

```
title 'Revenues for 1989';

proc print data=sasuser.regions noobs label;
    var region source deposit;
    label region='Chapter' source='Source'
            deposit='Contributions';
run;
```

```
                        Revenues for 1989                          1


                Chapter       Source    Contributions

                COASTAL       FEE          $1,000.00
                COASTAL       FEE          $9,337.67
                METRO         GIFT           $500.00
                METRO         FEE         $21,296.47
                METRO         GIFT         $5,000.00
                MOUNTAIN      FEE         $12,389.46
                UNIVERSITY    FEE         $10,005.15
```

Can You Calculate Totals?

You can obtain column totals.

The detail report might be more informative if it could show a total of all the funds deposited for the year. The PRINT procedure provides a SUM statement for requesting column totals for numeric variables simply by specifying the name of the variables you want summed.

Add a SUM statement to your PROC PRINT step, and you get the following report:

```
title 'Revenues for 1989';

proc print data=sasuser.regions noobs label;
    var region source deposit;
    label region='Chapter' source='Source'
          deposit='Contributions';
    sum deposit;
run;
```

A sum is printed for each variable you request.

```
                         Revenues for 1989                    1

              Chapter      Source   Contributions

              COASTAL      FEE          $1,000.00
              COASTAL      FEE          $9,337.67
              METRO        GIFT           $500.00
              METRO        FEE         $21,296.47
              METRO        GIFT         $5,000.00
              MOUNTAIN     FEE         $12,389.46
              UNIVERSITY   FEE         $10,005.15
                                       =============
                                       $59,528.75
```

What About Summary Reports?

Summary reports enable you to compute statistics and compare data by groups.

Summary reports generally appear in table form. Summary reports are valuable when you need to collapse data values into more meaningful information such as averages, counts, sums, and minimum or maximum values. You can group summary statistics to compare or present them.

The SAS System produces summary reports with procedure statements or with a windowing environment.

The REPORT procedure and the TABULATE procedure give you control over the appearance of reports and the type of statistics that appear in them. Both have a language component, but only the REPORT procedure provides two windowing interfaces—one that prompts you and one that allows you to use function keys and full-screen editing to design your report. In addition, using the REPORT procedure, you can create and store templates for reports you produce frequently.

The examples that follow show you two methods for producing a summary report of SASUSER.REGIONS. The first method uses the TABULATE procedure to produce a two-dimensional table with column and row totals. The second method shows you the results you obtain with the REPORT procedure.

How Do You Begin Creating a Table?

Determine the structure of your table.

The first step in preparing your summary table is to identify

☐ the categories by which you will group the data

☐ the statistics you want to show.

You might want to start by drawing a simple diagram and deciding which variables to put into it. The following diagram outlines a table for SASUSER.REGIONS.

	source	source	
region	sum	sum	total
region	sum	sum	total
	total	total	

Decide how you want to group your data.

Reports in table form generally present information in categories. The categories appear in the rows or the headings of your report and reflect the values of one or more variables. In SAS reporting procedures, these variables are called *class variables* or *grouping variables*. In the diagram above, the class variables are REGION and, within each value of REGION, SOURCE.

Decide how you want to summarize the data.

The diagram above shows the sum of the funds deposited for each source. In SAS reporting procedures, variables that are summarized or collapsed in this way are called *analysis variables*. You can also show means or other statistics for the analysis variables.

What Are the Steps in Building the Table?

Specify the class variables and the analysis variables.

In a CLASS statement, specify all the variables you want to use for grouping. The variables for which you want to compute statistics are listed in a VAR statement.

```
class region source;
var deposit;
```

Describe the table and specify the statistics.

You control these tasks with the TABLE statement. The TABLE statement below defines a two-dimensional table, that is, a simple table with rows and columns that fits onto one page. The comma in the TABLE statement separates the information about the rows (to its left) from the information about the columns (to its right). The following TABLE statement tells the TABULATE procedure to place the values of REGION in the rows of the table. Then it specifies that the columns should contain sums of the deposits, grouped according to the source.

The complete program for producing the table below looks like this:

```
proc tabulate data=sasuser.regions;
    class region source;
    var deposit;
    table region,deposit*source*sum;
run;
```

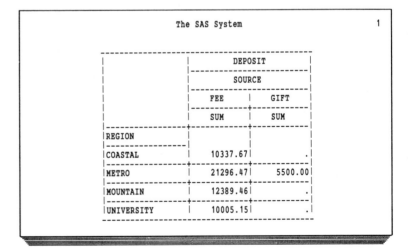

Can You Request Computed Values?

Ask for column totals.

The TABULATE procedure provides a universal class variable ALL that enables you to specify totals for rows and tables. The results you obtain depend on where you specify the variable.

In the following TABLE statement, specifying the variable ALL before the comma indicates that you want column totals. The TABULATE procedure sums all the rows.

```
table regions all,deposit*source*sum;
```

Ask for row totals.

The next TABLE statement indicates that the table should show row totals as well as column totals. For each row, you want to sum all the values of DEPOSIT.

```
table regions all,deposit*source*sum all*deposit*sum;
```

The following statements produce a table with row and column totals:

```
proc tabulate data=sasuser.regions;
    class region source;
    var deposit;
    table region all,deposit*source*sum all*deposit*sum;
run;
```

```
                              The SAS System                              1

            ---------------------------------------------------
            |                |            DEPOSIT             |         |
            |                |--------------------------------|         |
            |                |           SOURCE       |  ALL  |         |
            |                |------------------------|-------|         |
            |                |   FEE    |   GIFT   | DEPOSIT |         |
            |                |----------|----------|---------|         |
            |                |   SUM    |   SUM    |   SUM   |         |
            |----------------|----------|----------|---------|
            |REGION          |          |          |         |
            |----------------|          |          |         |
            |COASTAL         |  10337.67|        . |  10337.67|
            |----------------|----------|----------|---------|
            |METRO           |  21296.47|  5500.00 |  26796.47|
            |----------------|----------|----------|---------|
            |MOUNTAIN        |  12389.46|        . |  12389.46|
            |----------------|----------|----------|---------|
            |UNIVERSITY      |  10005.15|        . |  10005.15|
            |----------------|----------|----------|---------|
            |ALL             |  54028.75|  5500.00 |  59528.75|
            ---------------------------------------------------
```

How Can You Enhance Summary Tables?

Add titles and formats.   You can add titles and formats with the TITLE statement and the FORMAT= option of the PROC TABULATE statement. These features enable you to customize each report you prepare.

Change the headings in the table.   With the KEYLABEL and LABEL statements of the TABULATE procedure, you can change the variable name printed at the top of each column to a more meaningful heading. The following statements show you how to enhance your summary table with titles, formats, and labels.

```
title 'Revenues for 1989';

proc tabulate data=sasuser.regions format=15.2;
    class region source;
    var deposit;
    table region all,deposit*source*sum all*deposit*sum;
    keylabel all='Total';
    label region='Chapter' source='Source'
            deposit='Contributions';
run;
```

```
                                Revenues for 1989                          1

        ------------------------------------------------------------------
       |                 |             Contributions                      |
       |                 |------------------------------|                 |
       |                 |            Source            |     Total       |
       |                 |------------------------------|-----------------|
       |                 |    FEE     |     GIFT    | Contributions  |
       |                 |------------|-------------|-----------------|
       |                 |    SUM     |     SUM     |      SUM         |
       |-----------------|------------|-------------|-----------------|
       |Chapter          |            |             |                 |
       |-----------------|            |             |                 |
       |COASTAL          | $10,337.67 |          . |  $10,337.67    |
       |-----------------|------------|-------------|-----------------|
       |METRO            | $21,296.47 | $5,500.00  |  $26,796.47    |
       |-----------------|------------|-------------|-----------------|
       |MOUNTAIN         | $12,389.46 |          . |  $12,389.46    |
       |-----------------|------------|-------------|-----------------|
       |UNIVERSITY       | $10,005.15 |          . |  $10,005.15    |
       |-----------------|------------|-------------|-----------------|
       |Total            | $54,028.75 | $5,500.00  |  $59,528.75    |
        ------------------------------------------------------------------
```

Can You Produce Tables Interactively?

The REPORT procedure provides a windowing environment with a PROMPT facility that guides you through preparing a simple report.

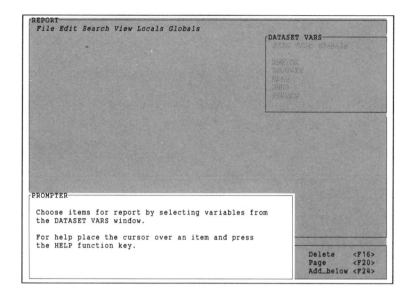

You have access to all the advanced features of the REPORT procedure through this windowing interface.

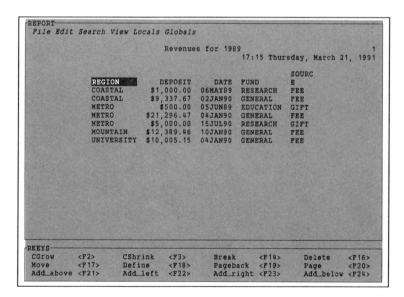

Can You Store Report Definitions?

You can store reports defined interactively or with program statements.

With the REPORT procedure, you can define a report and store the definition. The report definition can be used at another time to create the same report for any SAS data set that contains the variables in the report definition. This feature is available in both a windowing and nonwindowing environment.

You can produce a report of the data set SASUSER.REGIONS by submitting the following code.

```
proc report data=sasuser.regions headline headskip;
    title 'Revenues for 1989';
    col region source deposit;
    define region / group 'Chapter' width=15;
    define source / group 'Source' width=7;
    define deposit / sum 'Contributions'
            width=20;
    break after region / summarize ol skip suppress;
    rbreak after / dol summarize;
run;
```

Here is an example of a report defined with a few simple statements.

```
                          Revenues for 1989                        1

            Chapter        Source        Contributions
            ------------------------------------------------

            COASTAL        FEE               $10,337.67
                                         --------------------
                                             $10,337.67

            METRO          FEE               $21,296.47
                           GIFT               $5,500.00
                                         --------------------
                                             $26,796.47

            MOUNTAIN       FEE               $12,389.46
                                         --------------------
                                             $12,389.46

            UNIVERSITY     FEE               $10,005.15
                                         --------------------
                                             $10,005.15

                                         ====================
                                             $59,528.75
```

CHAPTER 6
Presenting Data with Graphics

With the SAS System's graphics capabilities, you can prepare charts
and plots for data analysis, or you can create color slides and graphics
for executive briefings. For simple line graphs, the graphical reporting
procedures, such as CHART and PLOT, produce clear, quick results.
For more polished presentations, you'll want the control and features
provided by PROC GCHART and other graphics procedures.

This chapter shows you simple programs for creating a vertical bar
chart using the SASUSER.REGIONS data set and showcases a few
sophisticated color graphs produced with SAS software.

What Are the Steps in Preparing a Simple Bar Chart?

Indicate which variable to chart. You indicate which variable to chart by naming the variable in the VBAR statement. For the chart in this example, REGION is a character variable so each bar represents one region.

Determine the statistic you want to calculate for the variable. You can request that the bars in your chart show the value of sums, averages, or frequency. To request a sum, you must specify SUM for the TYPE= option. If you want the bar to represent the total revenues for the year, specify DEPOSIT for the SUMVAR= option.

Decide if you want any grouping or subdividing. In this example, you show how much each source of income contributed to the total deposits for a region. If you add the SUBGROUP option, a different symbol is printed to represent the relative contribution of each source of income. In the chart below, the letter F represents the relative contributions from fees and the letter G represents contributions from gifts.

```
title 'Revenues for 1989';

proc chart data=sasuser.regions;
    vbar region / type=sum sumvar=deposit subgroup=source;
run;
```

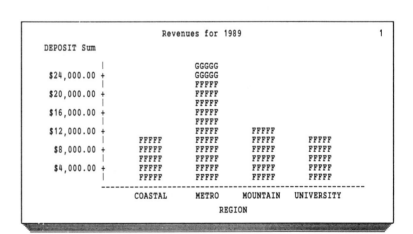

Can You Produce a More Polished Bar Chart?

Use graphics procedures.

To produce high resolution graphics, you use the GCHART procedure. Many of the GCHART statements are the same as the CHART procedure statements. The chart below is the same example you saw on the previous page, but the output is more polished because you used the GCHART procedure.

```
title 'Revenues for 1989';

proc gchart data=sasuser.regions;
    vbar region / type=sum sumvar=deposit subgroup=source;
run;
```

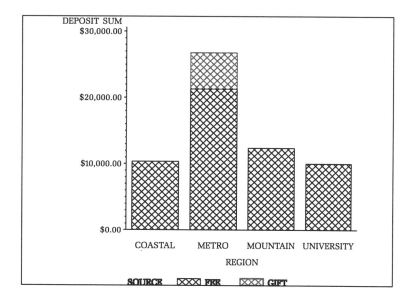

What Is Available for High Resolution Graphics?

The SAS System offers a variety of high resolution graphics procedures.

You create high resolution graphics by writing simple SAS programs such as the ones you've already seen in this chapter. Many of the high resolution and low resolution graphics have equivalent procedures. You can produce bar, block, and pie charts using the GCHART procedure. The GPLOT procedure enables you to present your data as a line plot, high-low plot, or scatter plot, and the G3D procedure creates surface plots. Four common types of maps are available through the GMAP procedure. You can generate simple text slides with the GSLIDE procedure. The GEDIT procedure enables you to modify your graphics output interactively.

The SAS System offers three methods of outputting your graphics images.

Once the graphics are created, you can

☐ display graphics on your monitor

☐ print graphics on a printer, slide camera, or plotter

☐ store graphics output.

The rest of the examples in this chapter show some of the graphics capabilities of the SAS System.

What Are Examples of Plots and Charts?

You can use the LEGEND statement to place a legend inside a plot.

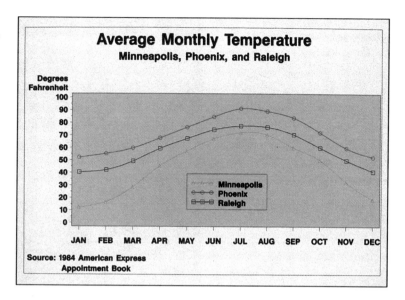

You can combine figures from the GCHART procedure using templates in the GREPLAY procedure.

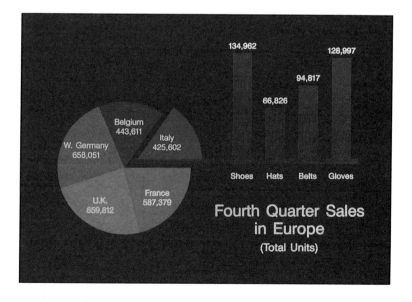

What are Examples of Maps?

You can combine maps with
other graphs.

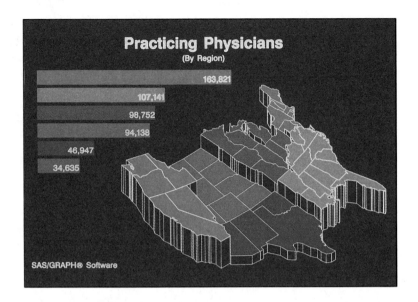

You can also overlay maps with
other graphs.

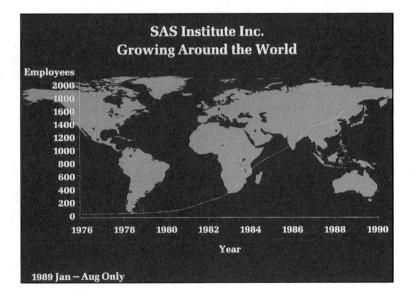

What Are Examples of Three-Dimensional Graphs?

You can produce three-dimensional scatter plots with the G3D procedure.

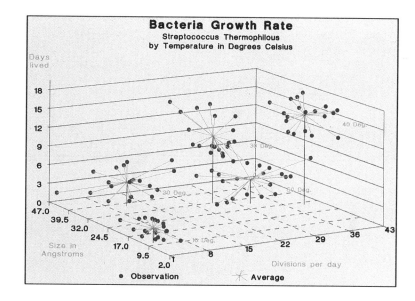

The G3D procedure also draws surface response figures.

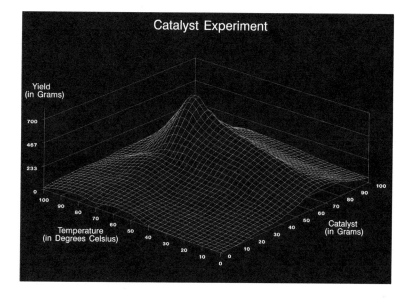

C H A P T E R   7
Building Applications

You've learned how easily the SAS System can

☐   read data from any source

☐   perform queries and manage data

☐   produce reports using lists, tables, and graphics.

Now you'll see how the applications development environment enables you to bundle all of these functions into a custom interface. This chapter briefly summarizes the tools available in the applications development environment.

Why Is an Applications Development Environment Important?

You can integrate data access, management, analysis, and presentation.

The SAS System enables you to use one software system to meet the diverse needs of all your users. With its complete functionality in data access, management, analysis, and presentation and its full spectrum of predefined applications, the SAS System can support any area of your business.

You can tailor applications to the level of computing expertise required by the user.

Your applications can give users quick, easy access to current information and enable both new and experienced users to utilize the SAS System without writing any programs. By making menu selections, users can produce reports, make ad hoc queries, submit production jobs, and even create graphics.

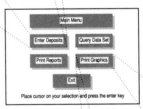

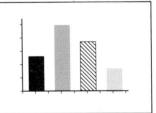

How Does the SAS System Provide an Applications Development Environment?

It offers a variety of development tools.

To develop applications, you must write SAS programs and provide a means for running them, often adding some way for the user to interact with the application as it runs. The ability to create customized, menu-driven applications is enhanced by a variety of tools:

- [ ] the ability to modify displays in the FSEDIT and FSVIEW procedures
- [ ] the BUILD procedure for creating displays
- [ ] a screen control language for managing the displays that make up an application and how they communicate with each other
- [ ] a macro language that stores and transfers text strings
- [ ] a full-screen application debugger
- [ ] an applications builder that enables you to build and link objects.

It enables you to add user-friendly features.

All the functions described in this book can be incorporated into custom applications that include many of the following features:

- [ ] menus that link the user to all parts of an application
- [ ] customized data entry screens that can validate the input
- [ ] selection lists and tables showing available choices
- [ ] help windows and prompts for the users
- [ ] computer-based training.

What Are Examples?

This is an example of a block menu created with the BUILD procedure and the screen control language.

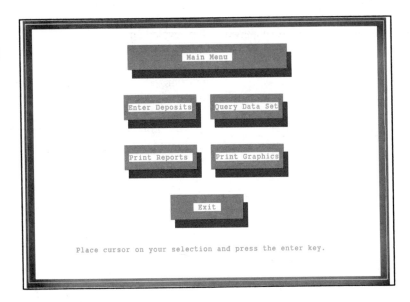

This is an example of a selection list for the tasks illustrated in this book. It was created with the BUILD procedure.

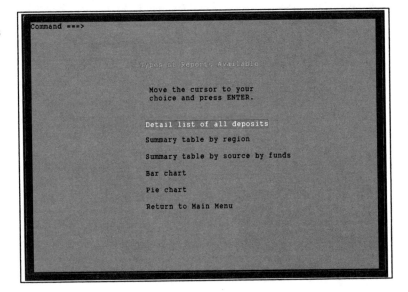

What's the Next Step in Learning the SAS System?

Publications

Now that you've seen how easy it is to use the SAS System, you'll want more information about the data access, management, and presentation features of the SAS System. Refer to these publications for a more detailed introduction and step-by-step instructions.

☐ *SAS Language and Procedures: Introduction, Version 6, First Edition*

☐ *SAS Language and Procedures: Usage, Version 6, First Edition*

☐ *SAS/GRAPH Software: Introduction, Version 6, First Edition*

For a complete listing of informative, up-to-date publications, consult the *Publications Catalog.*

Training

SAS Institute offers training to fit any topic or experience level. You can choose training for individuals or groups from three different media—instructor-based, video-based, or computer-based. Consult the *SAS Training* catalog for course offerings.

Technical Support

Technical support is provided free to all SAS System sites. Specialists are available to answer any questions you have about using the SAS System.

User Support

SAS Institute publishes a quarterly magazine, *SAS Communications*, which can keep you informed of the newest product features, additions to offerings in training and documentation, and stories of how other users are putting the SAS System to work in their organizations.

Index

Your Turn

If your have comments or suggestions about *Introducing the SAS System, Version 6, First Edition*, please send them to us on a photocopy of this page. Please return the photocopy to the Publications Division at SAS Institute Inc., SAS Campus Drive, Cary, NC 27513.

L.-Brault